Louisville
from A to Z

Liz Dumbaugh Martin, MSSW
Monte Edward Martin, MD

For Aiden and Mayzie, the twinkle in our eyes.

Special thanks to:
Della (Dumbaugh) Fenster, PhD, our cheerleader and family-based editor. To the rest of our family and friends, as they love Louisville as much as we do. And, to the Louisville Metro Department of Neighborhoods and photojournalist Jonathan Roberts, who assisted in our efforts to make this publication a reality. Jonathan saved us in the creative process by kindly sharing the photos for letters D, M & T.

A portion of the sale of this book will be contributed toward the restoration of the Preston Corridor and/or the Belmar Neighborhood Association, Inc. To learn more about them, visit www.bnainc.org.

Aa

is for:
Muhammad **Ali**,
Louisville's
three-time world
heavyweight
boxing
champion.

Bb

is for:

The **Belle** of Louisville, one of five remaining paddlewheel steamboats in the United States.

Cc

is for:
Churchill Downs, the most celebrated thoroughbred race track in the world.

Dd

is for:

Derby Day, the first Saturday in May, when three-year-old thoroughbred horses run the race that is known as "the fastest two minutes in sports."

Ee

is for:
Explorer– General George Rogers Clark established the first permanent settlement at the site that is now known as the City of Louisville.

 **is for:**

Fleur-de-lis—Louisville's city flag displays three gold fleurs-de-lis to recognize French assistance during the Revolutionary War.

Gg is for:
The "**Great** Balloon Race", where colorful "hound" balloons chase the "hare" balloon wherever the winds take them.

Hh

is for:
Henry's Ark, where orphaned animals find a home and children find new furry friends.

Ii

is for:
Iroquois Amphitheater, where families can enjoy music, plays and ice cream under the stars.

is for:

Jewelry, paintings, sculptures, and other handmade art for sale at the annual St. James Court Art Show.

Kk

is for:

The **Kentucky** Center for the Arts, where the orchestra performs while actors dance and sing.

Ll

is for:
Louisville Slugger,
the favorite bat of
major league
baseball for over
120 years.

Mm

is for:

Mini-Marathon, a 13.1 mile race for wheelchairs, walkers and runners, held during the Kentucky Derby Festival each year.

Nn

is for:

The many **neighborhoods** that make Louisville such a wonderful city in which to live.

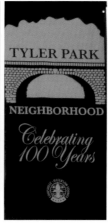

Oo

is for:

Frederick Law **Olmsted**, who designed Louisville's original parks system. He moved to Louisville after designing Central Park in New York City.

Preston Highway - Looking Southbound at Railroad Overpass
Existing Conditions   Perspective

Painted Railroad Bridge
w/ Welcome Sign

Terraced Railroad Enbankment:
Retaining Walls
Shrubs, ornamental grasses,
small flowering trees

Welcome to the
Preston Corridor

New Sidewalks
(Concrete or Pavers)

New
Curbs

Parkways with Grass
or groundcover and flowering bulbs

Preston Highway - Looking Southbound at Railroad Overpass
Conceptual Site Improvements   Perspective

Pp is for:
The **progress** made toward
beautifying older areas of the city.

Qq

is for:

Quito, the capital city of Ecuador and Sister City of Louisville.

Rr

is for:
Pee Wee **Reese**, a Louisvillian and Hall-of-Fame captain of the Brooklyn Dodgers. He helped Jackie Robinson, the first African-American baseball player, gain acceptance in the league.

Ss

is for:
The **Seelbach** Hotel, an historic Fourth Street landmark featured in the book, *The Great Gatsby*.

Tt

is for:

Thunder Over Louisville, the nation's largest annual fireworks display, and the official kickoff for the Kentucky Derby Festival each year.

Uu

is for:

The **University** of Louisville, home of the "Cardinals" and Louisville's oldest public college.

Vv

is for:
Victorian homes
that line the
streets of historic
Old Louisville.

Ww

is for:
The **Water** Tower
that marks the
spot where water
is pumped from
the Ohio River
into the city of
Louisville.

Xx

is for:
Louisville's **Xtreme** Park, which offers pipes, turns and spins for bikers, skateboarders and rollerbladers.

Yy

is for: **Yellow**, black, red, pink and blue cars that cruise Louisville's streets during the annual Street Rod Nationals.

Zz

is for:

The Louisville **Zoo**, where children ride the train and visit with more than 1,500 animals.